WHAT FRIDA SAYS

THE OFFICIAL COLLECTION

WHAT

FRIDA

SAYS

Hardie Grant

BOOKS

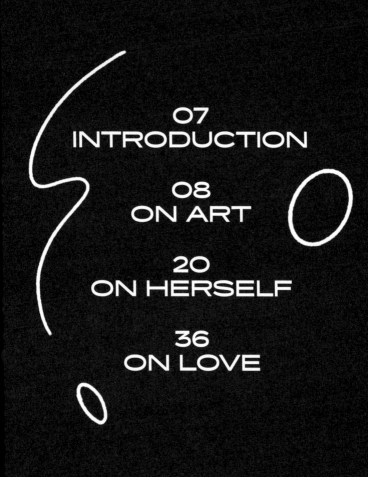

One of the most innovative and influential painters in history, Frida Kahlo is a legendary figure beloved the world over. Instantly recognisable for her unique style, she is also widely considered a fashion icon for her eclectic taste in clothing and jewellery, often mixing traditional Mexican attire with modern pieces. This love of colour and print translates into her acclaimed artwork, which she used throughout her life as an outlet for her physical and emotional pain.

Born in Coyoacán, Mexico in 1907, Frida overcame many difficulties, surviving polio as a child and battling lifelong injuries from a tragic road accident in her teens to become the inspirational figure we know today. The immense legacy of her art, dealing with themes of self-perception, love and loss, cannot be overlooked and her undeniable impact on popular culture continues to influence new generations.

Art

"My painting carries with it the message of pain."

"The only thing I know is that I paint because I need to, and I paint whatever passes through my head without any other consideration."

"I'll paint myself because
I am so often alone,
because I am the
subject I know best."

"Painting completed my life."

"They thought I was a
Surrealist, but I wasn't.
I never painted dreams.
I painted my own reality."

"To paint is the most <u>terrific</u> thing that there is, but to do it well is very difficult."

"I was born
a bitch.
I was born
a painter."

"I am not sick. I am broken. But, I am happy to be alive as long as I can paint."

"My paintings are the most frank expression of myself, without taking into consideration either judgements or prejudices of anyone."

"I don't know if my
paintings are Surrealist
or not, but what I am
sure of is that they
are the most honest
expression of my being."

On

Herself

"Feet, what do I need you for...

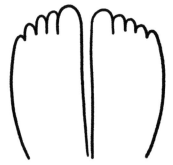

when I
have wings
to fly?"

"I tried to drown my sorrows, but the bastards learned how to swim, and now I am overwhelmed by this decent and good feeling."

"What doesn't kill me, nourishes me."

"I used to think I was the strangest person in the world, but then I thought, there are so many people in the world, there must be someone just like me who feels flawed and bizarre in the same ways I do…

I would imagine her, and
imagine that she must be
out there thinking of me too.
Well, I hope that if you are
out there and read this, know
that, yes, it's true I'm here, and
I'm just as strange as you." ♡

"I think
that
little by
little
I'll be able
to solve my
problems
and
survive."

"I already know everything,
without reading or writing.
Not very long ago, maybe
only a few days back, I was
a girl going her way through
a world of precise and
tangible colours and forms."

"The most important part of the body is the brain. Of my face, I like the eyebrows and eyes."

"I wish I could do whatever I
liked behind the curtain of
madness. Then: I'd arrange
flowers, all day long, I'd paint;
pain, love and tenderness,
I would laugh as much as
I feel like at the stupidity
of others and they would
all say: 'Poor thing, she's
crazy!' (Above all, I would
laugh at my own stupidity.)"

"I am female, but I have talent!"

"My blood
is a miracle
that, from
my veins,
crosses the
air from
my heart
to yours."

"Drink to forget, but now... I do not remember what."

"Whenever I speak with you,
I end up by dying more,
a little more."

On

Love

"Take a lover who looks at you like maybe you are a bourbon biscuit."

"Take a lover who looks at you like maybe you are magic."

"You deserve the best, the very best, because you are one of the few people in this miserable world who remain honest with others and that is the only thing that really counts."

"I leave you my portrait
so that you will have
my presence all the
days and nights that I
am away from you."

"I love you… thank
you because you live,
because yesterday you
allowed me to touch
your intimate light…

and because you
said with your voice
and your eyes
what I was waiting
for all my life."

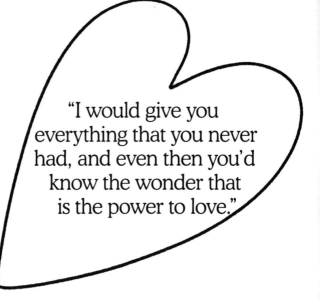

"I would give you everything that you never had, and even then you'd know the wonder that is the power to love."

"Love me
a little.
I adore
you."

On

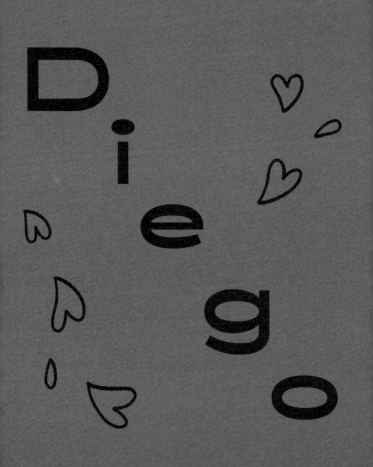

"Diego: <u>nothing</u> <u>compares</u>
to your hands, nothing like
the green-gold of your eyes.
My body is filled with you
for days and days. You are
the mirror of the night.
The violent flash of lightning.
The dampness of the earth…

The hollow of your armpits is
my shelter. My fingers touch
your blood. All my joy is
to feel life spring from your
flower-fountain that mine
keeps to fill all the paths of
my nerves which are yours."

"I cannot speak of Diego as my husband because that term, when applied to him, is an absurdity. He never has been, nor will he ever be, anybody's husband."

"You too know that all my eyes see, all I touch with myself, from any distance, is Diego. The caress of fabrics, the colour of colours, the wires, the nerves, the pencils, the leaves, the dust, the cells, the war and the sun, everything experienced in the minutes of the non-clocks and the non-calendars and the empty non-glances, is him."

"I saw Diego, and that
helped more than
anything else… I will
marry Diego again…
I am very happy."

"There have been two great accidents in my life. One was the train, the other was Diego. Diego was by far the worst."

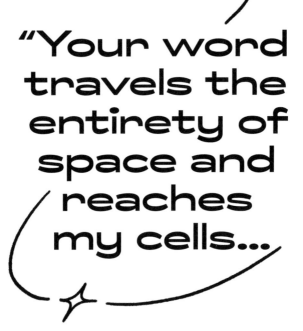

"Your word travels the entirety of space and reaches my cells...

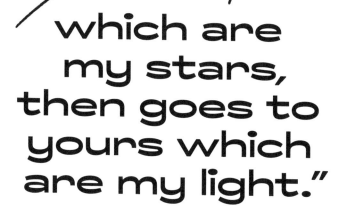

which are
my stars,
then goes to
yours which
are my light."

"All this anger has simply
made me understand
better that I love you <u>more</u>
than my own skin, and
that even though you
don't love me as much,
you love me a little
anyway – don't you?
If this is not true,
I'll always be hopeful
that it could be, and
that's enough for me."

"You took me in and gave me back broken, whole, complete."

"Your excessive passion wrapped me: the flames of the love were immense."

"You missed the opportunity to be happy."

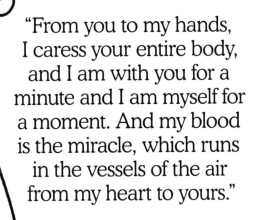

"From you to my hands,
I caress your entire body,
and I am with you for a
minute and I am myself for
a moment. And my blood
is the miracle, which runs
in the vessels of the air
from my heart to yours."

"I warn you that in this
picture I am painting
of Diego there will be
colours which even I am
not fully acquainted with.
Besides, I love Diego
so much I cannot be
an objective speculator
of him or his life."

"The most important thing for everyone in Gringolandia is to have ambition and become '<u>somebody</u>,' and frankly, I don't have the least ambition to become <u>anybody</u>."

"I find that Americans
completely lack sensibility
and good taste.
They are boring and
they all have faces
like unbaked rolls."

"It was worthwhile to
come here only to see
why Europe is rottening,
why all this people –
good for nothing –
are the cause of all the
Hitlers and Mussolinis."

"I am nauseated by all these
rotten people in Europe –
and these f*cking 'democracies'
are not worth even a crumb."

"I could kill that guy and eat it afterwards ..."

– in a letter to Nickolas Muray, discussing the Surrealists

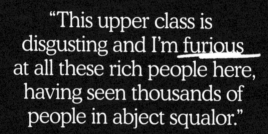

"This upper class is disgusting and I'm <u>furious</u> at all these rich people here, having seen thousands of people in abject squalor."

"Sometimes I prefer to talk to workers and bricklayers instead of those stupid people calling themselves educated people."

"They are
a bunch of
coo-coo,
lunatic, sons
of bitches
Surrealists."

"The devil is blonde
and his blue eyes,
like two stars fired love,
with his tie and red panties.
I think the devil is lovely."

"I would build my world which, while I lived, would be in agreement with all the worlds."

"Nothing is absolute.
Everything changes,
everything moves,
everything revolves,
everything flies
and goes away."

"There is nothing more precious than laughter."

"Only one
mountain can
know the core of
another mountain."

"Tragedy is
the most
ridiculous
thing."

"I hope the exit is joyful – and I hope never to come back."

"I must fight with all
my strength so that the
little positive things that
my health allows me
to do might be pointed
toward helping the
revolution. The only
real reason for living."

"Pain, pleasure and death
are no more than a
process for existence.
The revolutionary
struggle in this process
is a doorway open
to intelligence."

"It is not worthwhile to leave this world without having had a little fun in life."

"It is a strength to laugh and to abandon oneself, to be light."

"Doctor, if you let
me take this tequila,
I promise you not to
drink at my funeral."

"Beauty and ugliness
are a mirage,
because others end
up seeing what's
inside of us."

"I am in agreement with <u>everything</u> my <u>father</u> taught me and my <u>mother</u> taught me."

"Life is either a daring adventure or nothing."

"The pain is not part of the life,
but can be converted
into life itself."

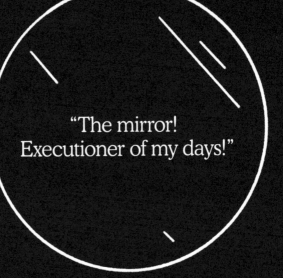

"The mirror!
Executioner of my days!"

"You have
to be honest;
we women
can not
live without
pain."

"What would I do without the absurd and the fleeting."

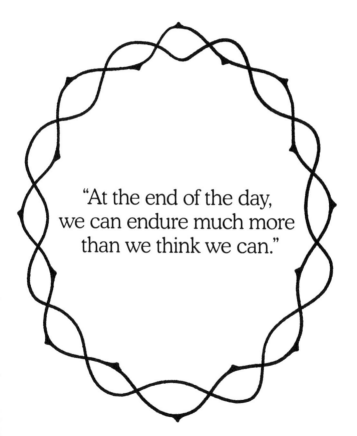

"At the end of the day,
we can endure much more
than we think we can."

SOURCES

Blago Kirov,
The Famous: Book 3,
Osmora Inc., 2014 –
p. 19, 24, 28, 31, 32, 33, 34,
35, 40, 42–43, 44, 50, 53,
57, 58, 59, 82, 85, 90, 91,
92, 93

Camilla Morton,
A Year in High Heels,
Hachette UK, 2011 – p. 41

Carol Sabbeth, *Frida Kahlo and
Diego Rivera: Their Lives and
Ideas*, Chicago Review Press,
2005 – pp. 17, 22–23

Carole Maso, *Beauty is
Convulsive: The Passion of
Frida Kahlo*, Counterpoint,
2002 – p. 60

Chrissie Grace, *Tiles Gone
Wild: New Directions in Mixed
Media Mosaics*, North Light
Books, 2008 – p. 11

David H. Lowenherz,
*The Greatest Love Letters of All
Time*, Crown, 2012 –
pp. 48–49

Diego Rivera, *My Art, My Life:
An Autobiography*, Courier
Corporation, 1960 -p. 61

Elizabeth Hess Stamper,
The Butterfly Book,
Balboa Press, 2016 – p. 39

Gerry Souter, *Frida Kahlo*,
Parkstone International, 2016 –
pp. 56, 68, 69

Hayden Herrera, *Frida Kahlo:
The Paintings*, Bloomsbury
Publishing, 1993 – p. 80

Helga Prignitz-Poda, Ingried
Brugger and Peter von Becker,
Frida Kahlo: Retrospective,
Prestel Verlag, 2010 –
pp. 54–55, 79

John Bloomberg-Rissman,
In the House of the Hangman,
Vol. 6, Lulu Press, 2017 –
pp. **64, 73**

Karla Clark, *Everybody and
Their Brother,* AuthorHouse,
2017 – p. **76**

Laura Barcella, *Fight Like a
Girl,* Summersdale Publishers,
2017 – pp. **29, 81**

Lawrence Tabak, *In Real Life,
Tuttle Publishing,* 2014 – p. **16**

Maria Tsenava, *Frida and
Diego: Quotes,* Lulu Press, 2013
– pp. **10, 13, 25, 38, 70, 71, 72,
86, 88, 89**

Sarah M. Lowe, *The Diary of
Frida Kahlo: An Intimate Self-
Portrait,* Abrams, 1995 –
pp. **51, 67, 77, 78**

Smithsonian Magazine,
November 2002 –
pp. **15, 65, 66, 83**

The Guardian,
21st May 2005 – p. **12**

Time Magazine,
27th April 1953 – p. **14**

Vanity Fair, 1995 – pp. **52, 87**

Victoria Brownworth, *Ordinary
Mayhem,* Bold Strokes Books
Inc., 2015 – pp. **26–27, 30**

Zena Alkayat and Nina
Cosford, *Frida Kahlo,*
Francis Lincoln Publishers,
2016 – pp. **18, 84**

Published in 2024 by Hardie Grant Books (London)

Hardie Grant Books (London)
5th & 6th Floors
52–54 Southwark Street
London SE1 1UN

hardiegrantbooks.com

British Library Cataloguing-in-Publication Data.
A catalogue record for this book is available from the
British Library.

What Frida Says
ISBN: 9781784887513

10 9 8 7 6 5 4 3 2 1

Publishing Director: Kajal Mistry
Editorial Director: Judith Hannam
Senior Commissioning Editor: Kate Burkett
Editorial Assistant: Harriet Thornley
Design and Art Direction: Double Slice Studio
(Amelia Leuzzi and Bonnie Eichelberger)
Production Controller: Martina Georgieva

Colour reproduction by p2d
Printed and bound in China by
RR Donnelley Asia Printing Solution Limited

MIX
Paper | Supporting
responsible forestry
FSC® C018179
FSC
www.fsc.org